Ranked in both Legal 500 and UK Chambers, Niall McCann undertakes all aspects of licensing and gaming and associated regulatory/planning law. He regularly appears as an advocate before courts and local authority sub-committees throughout England and Wales. He has lectured extensively on licensing matters and, in particular, specialises in advising on the impact of insolvency in respect of licensed premises.

Richard Williams is an experienced gaming, licensing and regulatory Solicitor, with over 20 years' experience of dealing with licensed premises nationally (including Scotland). Richard is a higher Courts advocate and regularly appears before Committees and Courts nationally, representing a full range of clients in the retail and leisure industries. He also specialises in food safety and health and safety law, particularly where this relates to licensed premises.

A Practical Guide to Licensing Law for Commercial Property Lawyers

A Practical Guide to Licensing Law for Commercial Property Lawyers

Niall McCann
LLB Hons
Partner and Joint Head of the Joelson Licensing,
Gambling and Regulatory Team

Richard Williams
LLB Hons and Solicitor Advocate
Partner and Joint Head of the Joelson Licensing,
Gambling and Regulatory Team

Law Brief Publishing

Published 2019 by Law Brief Publishing, an imprint of Law Brief Publishing Ltd
30 The Parks
Minehead
Somerset
TA24 8BT

www.lawbriefpublishing.com

Paperback: 978-1-911035-96-1

To Marilyn Gayle, Mia Wilson and Jonathan Beagle of the Joelson Licensing Team for all their support and assistance

PREFACE

This book is intended to be assist commercial property practitioners who handle transactions involving licensed properties. Given its length, it is merely an overview, but hopefully, one which highlights issues of importance and when to seek further specialist advice.

It does not explain how licensing regulation has evolved, opine on the potential impact of recent case law, nor does it reproduce large sections of the relevant legislation. There are already weighty tomes available, including the comprehensive Paterson's Licensing Acts, for those who wish to specialise in the area. This is not one of them.

Finally, unless otherwise stated, this book only applies to licensing in England and Wales and does not cover issues governed by complementary legislation, such as the Gambling Act 2005.

The law is up to date as of 1st December 2018.

Niall McCann
Richard Williams
December 2018

CONTENTS

CHAPTER ONE
LICENSING: THE BASICS

The Licensing Act 2003 (the "Act") is the principal statute covered by this book which came into force on 24 November 2005. Replacing the Licensing Act 1964, this product of the Blair years was designed to reduce regulation and devolve power to local authorities in order that they can shape their licensed economy. Decision making was moved from the Magistrates' Court to council committees and the rigid approach to the hours when licensable activity could take place was relaxed. No longer did bells in pubs always ring at 11.00 p.m. followed by the daily refrain of 'last orders please'! The success, or lack thereof, of this new approach has been debated both by academics and the press alike. It is not the intention of the authors to proffer an opinion but, what is clear, is that a considerable amount of regulation still remains and this flexible approach has not resulted in the 24-hour opening culture sometimes peddled by lazy pundits. Only a small percentage of premises have licences which permit alcohol to be sold 24 hours a day and the majority of these are large, out-of-town, supermarkets.

The Licensing Objectives

Four objectives underpin the Act:

- the prevention of crime and disorder;
- public safety;
- the prevention of public nuisance; and

- the protection of children from harm.

It is these that authorities seek to promote when authorising licensable activities or taking enforcement action. Any issue, concern, opinion or other matter raised by local residents, neighbourhood groups, the police, environmental health, councillors, members of parliament, businesses, trade bodies and the like, which do not relate to one or more of these objectives, is irrelevant under the Act. The wish to create employment: irrelevant. The promise of regeneration: irrelevant. Moral outrage: again, irrelevant.

> Are children under the age of 18 ever permitted to consume alcohol in licensed premises under any circumstances?
>
> Yes, but only 16 or 17 year olds, drinking beer, wine or cider, when accompanied by an adult and with a table meal.

What activity needs to be licensed?

A range of activity cannot be carried out in England and Wales unless specific permission has been granted. These activities include:

The Sale by Retail of Alcohol

Whilst seemingly obvious, even those with licensing experience can be confused with this licensable activity. It is the 'sale', not the consumption of alcohol, that is the licensable activity. Unless in a club setting, if alcohol is genuinely supplied free of charge a permission is not required: 'networking events', private parties and retail shops which supply complementary glasses of champagne to encourage customers to part with their money can all breathe a sigh of relief. Nevertheless, the alcohol does genuinely have to be suppled free of charge. The courts are alive to 'shams' whereby the price of other goods is inflated to compensate for the alcohol being free of charge. The most famous recent example was the Innsatiable in Farnham which, posing as a furniture shop, gave away alcohol (supposedly free of charge) but offered customers the chance to purchase beer mats. Following a legal battle, it closed.

Wholesale sales also do not require licensing permission. Therefore, provided importers of alcoholic drinks only supply to the trade and not the final consumer, they do not fall to be regulated as, ultimately, a permission will be required further down the supply chain.

A sale is deemed to have taken place where the alcohol is appropriated to the contract (i.e. the place the drink is taken from to be given to the customer). This could be a fridge or a barrel. Given this, a retail wine delivery merchant would not have to license the call centre but would need a permission for the warehouse from which orders are despatched. In some cases, it is not clear cut as to whether a licence is required or not. For example, what if a company imports Bordeaux directly from the vineyard, stores it in a warehouse in London before onward delivery to retail customers? In such a scenario, arguably a licence will not be required if the cases/bottles are allocated to customers before leaving the vineyard but will be required if the company 'buys in bulk' and only allocates the wine when it is in London and an order is placed.

Regulated Entertainment

Schedule 1 to the Act lists eight types of regulated entertainment, namely:

- A performance of a play.
- An exhibition of a film.
- An indoor sporting event.
- Boxing or wrestling entertainment.
- Performance of live music.
- Any playing of recorded music.
- Performance of dance.
- Entertainment of a similar description to that falling with performance of live music, any playing of recorded music or performance of dance.

Taking some of the key activities in turn, the following should be noted:

- A performance of a play

  Largely self-explanatory, the definition includes improvised works but not rehearsals. Plays have become less of a regulatory concern as recent deregulation now permits the performance of plays between 8.00 a.m. and 11.00 p.m. with an audience of up to 500 people without requiring a permission or licence.

- An exhibition of a film

A licence or permission is required for the showing of films, save for education purposes, those on live television, taking place in a place of worship, village hall etc. Incidental films, which could be the screening of silent films in a nightclub to add to the 'vibe', do not require a licence or permission.

For premises wishing to show films there are also other considerations (beyond the scope of this book) to consider matters such as copyright and age classification.

- An Indoor Sporting Event

The definition of a sporting event is one in which spectators are present. Therefore, snooker halls which merely provide tables for people to play against each other do not need to be licensed for indoor sporting events whereas, if they host competitions which attract an audience, this could be licensable. Indoor sporting events are now subject to a similar deregulation as that of plays, albeit that the maximum audience number can be 1000, rather than 500, before a licence is required.

- Boxing or Wrestling Entertainment

In a category all their own, any boxing or wrestling entertainment requires a licence except between 8.00 a.m. and 11.00 p.m. and for an audience of more than 1000 spectators. Bizarrely, Greco-Roman wrestling is specifically excluded and does not require a licence or permission. For fans of that sport, in the early 2000s things really couldn't get any better.

- Live and Recorded Music

The Licensing Act 1964 had a provision known as the 'two in a bar' rule which excluded the requirement to obtain a Public Entertainment Licence if two or fewer people were performing. This exemption was not adopted in the Act and, in what was a controversial move at the time, the playing of all live music, regardless of number of performers and recorded music requires a licence or permission. However, there were some concessions.

The definition of live and recorded music excludes live musical performances or the playing of recorded music which is incidental to a non-entertainment activity. What this means is a regular source of debate between operators, environmental health officers and enforcement bodies. Whilst there is no statutory test to determine whether music is incidental, there are two aspects which can be considered, namely, do a couple conversing have to raise their voices to be heard above the music and is the music the focus of the entertainment? If the answer is 'yes' to either it is likely that the music is licensable.

As with other forms of regulated entertainment, there has been some recent further deregulation. If a premises is licensed for the sale of alcohol it may play live and recorded music between 8.00 a.m. and 11.00 p.m. to an audience of up to 500 persons without these activities being permitted by the premises licence. This deregulation also suspended any conditions on a licence preventing such activity. A word of caution though; If the playing of music is a nuisance, operators can fall foul of other legislation and receive noise abatement notices or have premises licences reviewed (more of which later) and restrictions placed on a licence.

Late Night Refreshment

Late Night Refreshment is the supply of hot food and/or drink between the hours of 11.00 p.m. and 5.00 a.m. to members of the public. It does not have to be sold and can be for consumption either on or off the premises. This seemingly innocuous activity is licensed in order to bring late night takeaways into the licensing regime. The common belief is their presence can encourage late night revellers to stay out for longer, thus prolonging the risk of anti-social behaviour.

Whilst there are several exemptions (including for residents of hotels, staff canteens etc.), operators trying to argue that the food they supply is not sufficiently 'hot' to require licensing will not curry much favour – without a licence, late at night is the domain of the Frappuccino not the Cappuccino.

Decision Making

Whether or not to license or permit the above activities is determined by licensing authorities which, in the main, are district or borough councils, comprising ten to fifteen local councillors. They determine (whether directly or via delegated powers) applications by people or bodies wishing to carry out one or more of the above licensable activities by reference to the provisions of the Act and related statutory instruments, the council or borough's own licensing policy (which can usually be found online) and national guidance (again online – search for 'Section 182 Guidance').

More on how decision making works will be dealt with later in the book.

The Different Types of Permission

The Act introduced four types of permission:

Premises Licence

A premises licence attaches to a building or area, is generally capable of transfer from entity to entity, and permits one or more licensable activity, albeit usually with restrictions on hours and various conditions.

Personal Licence

Held by individuals, save for in community premises, only personal licence holders can make or authorise the sale of alcohol. Only personal licence holders can be designated premises supervisors – an individual named on a premises licence as the person authorised to sell or supply alcohol. Without a designated premises supervisor the supply of alcohol is not permitted pursuant to that premises licence. Common sense prevails and personal licence holders can, and do, delegate responsibility to sell alcohol to members of a licensed operation.

Club Premises Certificate

The permission required to supply or sell alcohol to members of a qualifying club and their guests. To be a qualifying club, amongst other things, a premises needs to have rules which determine membership, a two day interval between nomination/application and admittance and at least 25 members.

Temporary Event Notice

Effectively 'pop up' premises licences, temporary event notices ("TENs") can permit licensable activities to take place for up to a week at a time with up to 499 people attending at any one time. In total, a building or space may be covered by such notices for up to 21 days a year with at least 24 hours elapsing between TENs and a maximum of 15 TENs a year per building or space. Only the police or environmental health can object to a TEN. If they do, the notice is considered before a licensing sub-committee in much the same way as a new premises licence or variation application may (more of which later).

With the basic concepts of the Act outlined we move onto a more detailed analysis of the most important permission of them all: the premises licence.

CHAPTER TWO
THE PREMISES LICENCE

What does a premises licence permit?

As mentioned in Chapter 1, a premises licence permits licensable activities to be carried out in a building or area to the extent permitted by the hours, licensable activities and conditions recorded on the premises licence.

How long do they last for?

Most premises licences are granted to last in perpetuity. Occasionally they are only granted for a finite period, for example to license a 'one off' summer music festival or 'pop up' restaurant.

Premises licences will only cease to be if surrendered, revoked following a review application or if they lapse due to insolvency of the holder. The latter two triggers are given more attention in subsequent chapters.

Are premises licences renewed?

It is a common misconception that premises licences need to be renewed annually. They do not. However, an annual fee is payable based on the rateable value of the licensed premises. The fee band currently ranges from £100 to £1905. If the fee is not paid in a timely manner the premises licence can be suspended until the debt is paid.

Who can apply for a premises licence?

Premises licence can be held by any person who carries out, or proposes to carry out, licensable activity. A person includes an individual, partnership or corporate entity and no legal interest in the premises in question is required. Carrying or proposing to carry out licensable activity is interpreted broadly. In *Hall & Woodhouse v Poole Brough Council [2010] 1 All ER 425* it was held that even a landlord could satisfy this test. In reality, councils rarely investigate the licence holder's ability to carry on licensable activities unless there are concerns in respect of the premises' operation.

How are premises licences granted?

Applications are made to the local council or borough in which the building or space is located. Most councils now accept online applications, and many have their own bespoke forms. All applications must include:

- The details of the applicant, the hours and licensable activities sought, whether any sale of alcohol is to be for on or off the premises or both and an explanation of how the applicant proposes to uphold the four licensing objectives.

- A plan drawn up pursuant to the requirements of the Licensing Act 2003 (Premises Licences and Club Premises Certificates) Regulations 2005 which accurately depicts the layout of the proposed licensed area.

- The payment of an application fee which is the same amount as the annual fee.

- If the premises licence is to permit the sale of alcohol, the consent of the proposed designated premises supervisor.

Is there a formal preapplication consultation process as in planning? Whilst not as common as in planning applications, it is usually possible to take preapplication advice. Some councils have a formal service (for a fee) whereby a licensing officer will visit the site, discuss the proposals and produce a report. Where such a service is not advertised it might still be possible to have an informal discussion or meeting with officers.

Once lodged, an application must be served on a list of statutory authorities which, if made electronically, is fortunately the responsibility of the licensing authority.

Applications are required to be advertised in two ways. Firstly, by the display for a continuous period of 28 days of an A4 notice on light blue paper on, or near, the site in question and the publishing of a notice in a local newspaper or newsletter. Both requirements have strict technical requirements which, if not followed to the letter, can invalidate the application.

Does anyone actually read advertisements in local papers? Rarely. Most representations made by local residents are because the blue notice on site is read or the council has informed

nearby residents by post. There is nothing which prevents an applicant from putting up a more detailed description of the application next to the blue notice, so residents have a better overall picture before deciding whether, or not, to object.

Beginning the day after the application is made, there is a 28-day consultation period in which relevant representations may be made. A relevant representation is one made by a responsible authority (such as the police, environmental health or the licensing authority itself) or other person (such as a nearby resident) which comments on the likely effect of the grant of a premises licence on one or more of the licensing objectives. Typically, residents' concerns focus upon noise nuisance and anti-social behaviour such as public urination and litter which can stem from heavy drinking. Issues such as the damaging health effects of excessive alcohol consumption, morality concerns or residents' parking are either irrelevant or covered by other legislation. Such arguments should not be given much truck by licensing authorities. To be relevant, representations cannot be frivolous or vexatious.

Are late representations admissible?

No. This was confirmed in *Corporation of the Hall of Arts and Sciences v The Albert Court Residents Association and ors [2011] EWCA Civ 430*. However, many authorities are reluctant to confirm the grant of an application until handwritten letters, potentially delivered on time, have reached the correct officer.

If no relevant representations are made in the consultation period the application is automatically granted, as sought, by way of delegated authority on the 29th day. If relevant representations are made and maintained the application must be determined before a licensing sub-committee within 20 working days of the last date for representations, albeit that this period can be extended if required.

Licensing sub-committee hearings are quasi-judicial and should take the form of a discussion led by the authority which, in most cases, is a panel of three councillors with one acting as chair. The formality of such hearings vary from council to council and the nature of the application and representations. An application to license a small café which only attracts one, rather dubious, representation from a local rival will normally be granted after only a few minutes of submissions and questioning, whereas an application made on behalf of a proposed nightclub could attract hundreds of representations including from the statutory authorities, thus generally necessitating a lengthy hearing with detailed legal and factual arguments presented by specialist licensing solicitors or barristers representing both the applicant and the objectors. However, some councils stipulate a maximum time to make oral submissions which can be as short as five or ten minutes. This can be incredibly frustrating when an application is nuanced, complicated or requires detailed legal submissions.

> Do only solicitors or barristers have rights of audience to appear on behalf of applicants?
>
> No, anyone can represent an applicant. There are many licensed 'consultants' (often ex-police or licensing officers) that appear on behalf of clients. Also, applicants can, and do, represent themselves. This is not recommended when the applicant is an inexperienced operator.

Where the application is complicated, or time limits prevail, prior to a licensing sub-committee it is often prudent to serve the objectors and council with evidence on which the applicant wishes to rely. This could range from something as simple as an indicative drinks list to full blown witness statements with copious exhibits. Application forms for news premises licence are rather formulaic and, without serving prior evidence, it can be difficult to sufficiently make a case by way of oral submissions. Permission to serve evidence prior to a hearing is not required. Evidence produced at a hearing is only admissible if all parties agree to its use.

The licensing committee may grant in full or in part or refuse an application altogether with an interested party being able to appeal the decision to the Magistrates' Court within 21 days of the written decision. Most decisions to grant premises licences are not appealed by aggrieved local residents or statutory bodies, even if the application was hotly contested. The main reason why this is the case is that, on appeal, costs awards may be made. When weighing up the risks posed by a newly licensed premises or possibly having to pay an operator's legal fees if an appeal is unsuccessful, local residents usually perceive the former to be the lesser of the two evils. Appeals are more likely to be made by aggrieved operators who had an application refused or only granted in part. Such appeals are often compromised long before the substantive appeal hearing to avoid legal fees and the risks of losing.

Does mediation not have a role to play?

It does but is not nearly as prevalent as in civil litigation. For example, Southwark Council pays for a mediation service, where applicable, both before and after applications are made and several high-profile practitioners, including the authors, support its greater use. The stumbling block is one of cost. In commercial civil disputes both parties are usually happy to share the costs of the mediator in the hope that legal fees can be saved in the long run. With licensing matters, local residents do not expect to pay legal fees and operators are reluctant to pay greater legal fees than they expected to incur. Whilst more councils might start to pay for a mediation service, they will only do so if convinced that enough time and money can be saved from having fewer or truncated licensing sub-committee hearings.

CHAPTER THREE
ACQUIRING LICENSED PREMISES

Too often, commercial property practitioners treat the acquiring of licensed premises no differently to that of an office block, warehouse, or standard retail unit. This can be disastrous as the fact a premises is licensed can equate to a significant part of its rev value. Some clients prefer to instruct specialist lawyers or (unwisely) handle the licensing matters themselves. In such cases, it goes without saying that the ambit of the instructions needs to be clear in the engagement letter.

So what steps should practitioners take to protect their clients?

Study the premises licence in detail

A copy of the latest premises licence should be sought from the vendor. Most councils do have online registers which provide either the key aspects of the licence or copies of the licences themselves, but they are not full proof. Such portals are only as accurate as the person inputting the data. Every council has a 'house style' and this will dictate the look of the premises licences they produce. However, all premises licences record the following:

Name of the premises licence holder

An obvious point, but one often overlooked, is that it is vital to know who the licence holder is. Not only do they control what can be a very valuable asset but a change in the holder's circumstances could see the licence lapsing (more of which in chapter 4).

Hours for licensable activities

All the permitted licensable activities and the hours they apply should be clearly shown. However, there might be some seasonal variations such as New Year's Eve or the Sundays before bank holidays. The opening times will often be shown. As opening hours is not a licensable activity, their enforceability, especially in respect of early opening, is debatable.

> Do all premises have 30 minutes 'drinking up' time?
>
> No. Pursuant to the Licensing Act 1964 pubs had 20 minutes. 30 minutes has now become popular as many consider it the correct balance between avoiding patrons having to 'down' drinks, thus adding to intoxication, whilst avoiding the 'stockpiling' of drinks immediately prior to the terminal hour for the sale of alcohol.

The designated premises supervisor

Their name, personal licence number and issuing authority will be on the premises licence. If the designated premises supervisor is to leave the business or is going to be absent from work for a prolonged period, a designated premises supervisor variation application will have to be made to the local authority on completion to appoint a replacement.

Conditions

All premises licences have a list of conditions which control and curtail licensable activity. They are either:

- mandatory conditions which are placed on all premises licences (such as not allowing irresponsible promotions to be carried out);

- conditions which were proffered by an applicant before the premises licence was granted; or

- conditions placed on the premises licence following a licensing sub-committee hearing.

Conditions are not merely advisory. Failure to comply with them is a criminal offence and could lead to prosecution or a review application being made. What is more, whilst some councils (such as the City of Westminster) have a pool of model conditions they adopt, there are no 'set' conditions for pubs, bars, restaurants and the like. They are often 'free drafted' and hence the range of conditions are endless.

Practitioners should study conditions closely to ensure they do not adversely restrict the proposed style of operation. Typical onerous conditions include a requirement:

- for all consumption of alcohol to be with a substantial meal;

- to employ door supervisors (the technical term for a 'bouncer');

- to close a beer garden early;

- to limit the capacity;

- not to have off sales for immediate consumption (i.e. drinking on the pavement outside a pub);
- to only serve drinks in polycarbonate vessels; or
- to control the volume of music.

Onerous conditions are explored in more detail in chapter 5.

What if a condition is clearly meaningless or relates to repealed legislation?

Whilst enforcement action should not be taken in such circumstances it might be prudent to remove such conditions by way of a minor variation application.

The Layout Plan

As part of the premises licence, the layout plan must be an accurate reflection of the actual layout itself. A criminal offence is being committed if licensable activities continue to be carried out until a variation application is granted. The difficulty is that the inaccuracy of plans often only come to light when the business is being sold, where there is an inspection from one or more of the statutory authorities or a variation of a different variety is being contemplated, i.e. whilst the premises is trading. So, what happens in such circumstances? Strictly speaking the premises should close until the anomaly is rectified. In practice, many operators take the pragmatic (if slightly risky) approach of ignoring the inconsistency (if possible) until the premises is next closed for refurbishment or lodging a variation of layout application and hoping that a 'blind eye' will be turned.

The cautious practitioner will ask their client to confirm that the plan is accurate.

> Do plans have to be in a prescribed form?
>
> Yes, they do. The Licensing Act 2003 (Premises licences and club premises certificates) Regulations 2005 lists the requirements. However, approved plans will often fall short of these requirements, especially when prepared during the transitional period in 2005 when councils were too hard pressed to refuse slightly defective applications.

Send out specific licensing pre-contract enquiries

It is insufficient to rely on standard pre-contract enquiries when acquiring licensed premises. Whilst there is no standard form that the licensing enquiries should take, examples are at appendix A.

Prima facie, some of these enquiries appear irrelevant. Why should it matter if there has been a review application when the operation is to change hands? Well, it could be that more than poor management is to blame. Structural issues, overly sensitive residents or a change to the local demographic can all spell problems for a future operator. There are pockets in each major town and city which are renowned for having particularly difficult residents. Nimbyism can be rife and if residents have complained about a licensed premises in the past they are likely to do so again, even if the style of operation changes for the better. Furthermore, unlike in planning law, licensing has not, at the time of writing, adopted the 'agent of change' principle. Even if someone buys a house next door to a historic pub they can still apply to review its premises licence if they are being disturbed.

The same rational applies to past prosecutions. A new operator can be tarred with an old operator's brush. For example, if an operator has previously been prosecuted for under age sales, it could be more likely that further test purchases are carried out. Test purchases are one of the few examples of entrapment in English and Welsh law. Statutory bodies such as the police and trading standards can send minors into licensed premises where they ask to purchase alcohol drinks. If the member of bar staff either fails to ask for identification or asks for identification (which cannot be provided) and serves the minor anyway, the test purchased has been failed. This usually results in the issuing of a fixed penalty notice and can lead to a prosecution or review application, especially if the premises is a repeat offender. It is all too easy for bar staff in a busy premises to fail test purchasers and the authorities will not necessarily take into account that previous offences were committed by a different operator.

Do members of bar staff really serve underage people these days?

They often do when test purchasing is conducted. A confident 16-year old walking to the bar with a note in hand knowing that they are doing nothing wrong gives off a completely different air to the nervous teen pushed forward by their friends on the basis that they are the tallest in the group!

Other forms of due diligence

If a 'high risk' premises such as a nightclub or late-night bar is being acquired it might be prudent if the operator or its solicitor makes enquiries of the statutory authorities. Not only can they verify the answers to the pre-contract enquiries, but useful information can be gleaned and valuable relationships formed. For example, a nightclub might never have been at the receiving end of a review application but, a simple chat to the local police licensing sergeant could reveal a litany of concerns and early warning of a pending review application.

Steps required to be taken on completion

Transferring the premises licence

The required licensing provisions in an Agreement for Lease where completion is subject to licensing is explored in a separate chapter. For a straightforward acquisition the required steps on completion are relatively simple. The vendor should provide the original premises licence and a consent to transfer signed by the outgoing premises licence holder.

On completion, the assignee or purchaser's solicitor should apply to transfer the premises licence providing a copy of the signed consent. Such applications are relatively simple and can usually be completed online. They are effective immediately, save for a chief officer of police can object if they are satisfied that the exceptional circumstances of the case are such that granting the application would undermine the crime prevention objective. Objections are very rare.

It is important that transfer applications are made as soon as reasonably practicable after completion. If not, there is a risk from the vendor/assignor's perspective that they could still be liable for actions outside of their control and, for an assignee/purchaser, there is the risk that the vendor/assignor will surrender the premises licence or seek to withdraw its consent to the transfer.

It can happen that consent to transfer cannot be obtained. The premises licence holder might have moved away, or a legal dispute could mean that consent is actively not given. In such circumstances a transfer application will still be processed provided that all reasonable steps have been taken to obtain the consent to transfer. Whilst dependent on the facts, the council will probably want a detailed account of the circumstances and evidence that consent has been sought.

Sometimes the vendor is unable to provide the original premises licence. Although it is a legal requirement to keep the original premises licence or a certified copy on site, all too often they are mislaid. Alternately, the latest version may still not have been produced by the council following the grant of an application to vary the licence. The transfer application should explain why the original premises licence is missing. If it has been mislaid, the council might ask for payment of £10.50.

Varying the designated premises supervisor

If the designated premises supervisor named on the premises licence is to leave the business, an application to vary the designated premises supervisor is required. As with a transfer application it is a straightforward process and deemed effective as soon as lodged. The consent of the incoming designated premises supervisor is required, and the original premises licence supplied.

Further varying the premises licence

If a turnkey operation no further steps are necessary. However, if the layout, licensable activities, hours or conditions need to be changed then an application to vary the premises licence is required.

Applications to amend the deposited plans are generally the most straightforward. For changes of layout which involve small alterations to structure or layout which do not increase the size of the licensed area, the minor variation procedure may usually be used. Such applications only attract a fee of £89.00, do not have to be advertised save for display of a white notice and are determined within 15 working days of being lodged.

For more substantial refurbishments and variations to hours, activities or relevant conditions the full variation process is required. This process is almost identical to that of applying for a new premises licence as described in chapter 2.

> What if it is marginal as to whether a minor or full variation is required?
>
> This is a common problem. A helpful licensing officer might provide guidance on the telephone or by email. If not, it really depends on timing. If there is time for the minor variation to be rejected and a full variation determined this could be an option. Otherwise, it might be safer to simply lodge a full variation. If time is very tight there might not be any other option but to lodge a minor variation and apply for some Temporary Event Notices in case it is rejected.

CHAPTER FOUR
THE IMPACT OF INSOLVENCY

If one was to read only one chapter from this book it should be this one. A lack of understanding as to how insolvency affects licensed premises is a common form of negligence amongst property practitioners. This is because section 27 of the Act stipulates that a premises licence will lapse if the holder:

- dies;
- becomes a person who lacks capacity;
- becomes insolvent;
- is dissolved; or
- if it is a club, ceases to be a club.

The third of these bullet points is the focus of this chapter.

How is insolvency defined?

For the purposes of an individual, insolvency is:

- the approval of a voluntary arrangement approved by him;
- being adjudged bankrupt or having his estate sequestrated; or

- entering into a deed of arrangement made for the benefit of his creditors or a trust deed for his creditors.

A company is insolvent on:

- the approval of a voluntary arrangement proposed by its directors;
- the appointment of an administrator in respect of the company;
- the appointment of an administrative receiver in respect of the company; or
- going into liquidation.

> What if the premises licence is held by a husband and wife and only one is adjudged bankrupt? Does the premises licence still lapse?
>
> This question is still to be thoroughly tested in the courts. In such cases a cautious approach should be taken and the premises licence transferred into the sole name of the person not adjudged bankrupt (see below).

Often practitioners are surprised to learn that voluntary arrangements (typically known as IVAs and CVAs respectively) fall within the definition of insolvency given that these are essentially 'deals' made with creditors seemingly to *avoid* 'full blown' insolvency. Conversely, the appointment of an LPA Receiver where a borrower has defaulted on a mortgage does not fall within the Act's definition of insolvency.

So when, precisely, does insolvency take place?

This will depend on the type of insolvency. It could be the granting of a court order, the date of appointment etc. The instructed insolvency practitioner should be asked to advise.

When does a premises licence lapsing following insolvency?

Immediately upon the holder of the premises licence becoming insolvent the premises licence lapses and it becomes illegal to carry out any licensable activities until it is, if ever, reinstated. A person found guilty of carrying out licensable activities without the benefit of a premises licence faces up to six months imprisonment and/or an unlimited fine. Whilst it is unlikely that anyone would be imprisoned for serving a few pints after an IVA had been agreed, these severe sanctions should focus the mind.

Do the authorities ever turn a 'blind eye'?

The approach taken varies enormously. The authors have heard of police raids, proprietors being led away in handcuffs and other unwelcome measures. Examples at the other end of the spectrum include transfers being permitted out of time (see below) and overlooking certain types of insolvency. It often cannot be said whether these examples are deliberate oversights or based on a lack of legal understanding.

How can a premises licence be reinstated?

A lapsed premises licence can be reinstated provided that either an interim authority notice ("IAN") or transfer is lodged within 28 days of the lapse.

An IAN application can be made by someone with a prescribed interest in the premises or who is a connected person who held the premises licence immediately before its lapse. In other words, an insolvency practitioner or someone involved in running the business. As with a transfer, an IAN application is made to the local authority in which the premises is located and is effective immediately. It reinstates the premises licence but only for a period of up to three months. If, during this three-month period, the premises licence is then not transferred, it will once again lapse, this time permanently.

The transfer option is permanent (provided of course that the new holder does not become insolvent). The process is described in the previous chapter but, crucially, consent of the outgoing holder is not required. When the business is not to be immediately sold (i.e. pre-packed) a transfer can be made in the name of a new co. holding company, another company in the group which has not become insolvent, an individual connected to the business or a specialist third party instructed to run the business whilst a buyer is found.

Whichever process is followed, it is important that there is no delay between the insolvency 'trigger' and an application being made. In the case of a transfer, it might be possible to transfer a licence before insolvency takes place.

Which option is preferable?

Given that both transfer and IAN application are effectively immediately and relatively straightforward, usually it is sensible to apply for the former given that it permanently reinstates the licence. Insolvency Practitioners are particularly suspicious of IANs as they confer personal liability on the appointment taker which is never welcome. The IAN route is principally taken when the premises are not going to trade, a quick sale is likely and there is no obvious other entity to hold the premises licence in the intervening period.

How does this affect property lawyers?

Save for being a good advisor to an ongoing client (it is surprising as to how many insolvency practitioners are ignorant of the effects of their advice on licensed property) a knowledge of how a premises licence can lapse is essential when acting for a client looking to acquire a licensed property to ensure that the proper enquiries are made (see chapter 2). The relevant questions should form part of the pre-contact enquires and, if the holder of the premises licence is an individual, a bankruptcy search should be carried out and, if a company, companies house should be consulted.

Can reinstating a company 'reverse' the lapse?

In *Beauchamp Pizza Ltd v. Coventry City Council [2010] EWHC 926 (Ch)* it was held that if a premises licence is held by a company which is struck off the register and dissolved, but subsequently restored to the Register, the company shall be 'deemed to have continued in existence as if its name had not been struck off'.

What are the consequences of inadvertently acquiring a premises where the premises licence has irrevocably lapsed?

The purchaser will have acquired a very expensive juice bar. On a more serious note, the best outcome is that there is simply a delay in being able to carry out licensable activities for a period whilst an application for a new premises licence is being consulted upon. A series of TENs (see chapter 1) may be applied for provided that the annual quota has not already been used. This is not a perfect solution as a premises can only be covered for twenty one days, a day's gap is required between each TEN and at least five working days' notice is required to be given (in the case of a short notice TEN) before any licensable activity can take place. On days when the premises is not covered by a TEN, it can still open provided that no licensable activity takes place. For example, a fine dining restaurant might choose to open but supply house wine free of charge to patrons to avoid the inevitable loss of goodwill that temporary closure could bring.

Even if an application for a new premises licence is made on the same terms as the lapsed licence, there is no guarantee the application will be granted as sought, if at all. Operations on the brink of insolvency often 'push the boundaries' in order help the bottom line. For example, the numbers of door supervisors might be reduced which hampers supervision or drinks prices slashed encouraging a larger and more boisterous crowd. Such steps can impact upon the licensing objectives and antagonise the statutory authorities and local residents. They might not be too keen on the grant of a new premises licence and raise persuasive representations. This is especially so in cumulative impact zones where new licences are not granted on the same terms as those that have been in existence for years.

Save for potential loss of trade, there are cost implications when applying for a new premises licence – not just legal fees, but architects' fees for drawing up plans, advertisement fees and also the council application fee itself. If a property practitioner has failed to adequately check whether a premises licence remains in force the damages sought by a disgruntled client can be significant.

How do councils find out that a premises licence has lapsed?

Whilst it varies from council to council, many undertake regular checks of Companies House. Others will check when an application is received. Some are even 'tipped off' by other operators.

CHAPTER FIVE
CONDITIONAL CONTRACTS AND NEW DEVELOPMENTS

Where a unit is unlicensed, but one is required by a new tenant, the responsibility of having a premises licence granted is often left to the tenant. This is a logical approach. The unit might be advertised as suitable for a variety of uses. Why should the landlord waste time and money securing a premises licence which may not be required? Conversely, a proposed tenant will know the form any application should take and should be able to commission accurate layout drawings. The challenge is that landlords want the certainty of knowing a unit will be let, whereas potentially tenants do not want to commit to a lease without the comfort of having a suitable premises licence. The answer is having an Agreement to Lease which requires the proposed tenant to complete a lease in an agreed form provided that a premises licence is granted which is free of onerous conditions.

There is no standard wording a practitioner can simply 'cut and paste' into a precedent Agreement for Lease. Nevertheless, there is usually a separate clause or schedule which deals with licensing matters. One would expect the following aspects to be covered:

- A definition of what is an 'onerous condition'. This will depend on the proposed style of operation, the negotiating powers of the respective parties and the location of the unit. Typical examples of onerous conditions include –
    - Having to cease licensable activities or close before a certain time.

This is the most important condition. For example, a pub which has to stop serving before 11.00 p.m. Monday to Saturday and 10.30 p.m. on Sunday is unlikely to be successful. Whilst there is not prescribed statutory 'drinking up time', 30 minutes is common, in which case, if the minimum acceptable hour for the end of licensable activities is 11.00 p.m., the respective minimum acceptable closing time should be 11.30 p.m. For the avoidance of doubt, any closing time stipulated on a premises licence refers to members of the public. Unless there is a relevant condition, staff, cleaners etc. can be on site after closing time.

- A requirement that the consumption of alcohol must be ancillary to food.

Another important consideration and a very common requirement on premises licences granted within cumulative impact zones. Any condition that the sale or consumption of alcohol must be ancillary to food precludes bar or pub use. 'Food' or 'substantial food' is not defined but there is a plethora of case law stemming from the Licensing Act 1964. It does not include crisps, nuts or olives! The food does not have to be paid for but, in practice, it is unrealistic for operators to provide food free of charge to customers who do not order it.

Whilst all conditions on a premises licence must be adhered to, requirements that alcohol must be ancillary to food is enforced albeit that licensing officers usually take a common-sense approach. If, for example, a couple take a seat, order expensive drinks and then decide that the menu is not to their liking and ask to leave, few would take issue with payment being taken. Likewise, where there is a large group and one of the guests decides not to eat, enforcement action is unlikely. As a licensing officer once said to the authors, 'when I walk into a premises I instantly know if it is operating as a restaurant or bar'. What is more of a grey area is when restaurants have holding bars. In such circumstances, if a patron has a cocktail in the bar but only consumes food an hour later in the restaurant area, was the consumption of the cocktail ancillary to food? It's a debateable point and one which can turn on the exact wording of any condition. For the avoidance of doubt, with restaurants that have holding bars in the City of Westminster, usually there is a condition that the consumption of alcohol must be ancillary to food save for a certain number of covers which can be for patrons having pre, and sometimes post, dinner drinks. In any case, requirements that food must be consumed with alcohol do not necessarily curb alcohol fuelled nuisance. There is a greater likelihood of high jinks from a group enjoying numerous bottles of wine over a boozy lunch than those having a quick pint before catching the train home.

- Requires patrons to be seated and/or alcohol to be supplied by waiter/waitress service.

  Although not as fundamental to a business as a requirement that the consumption must be with food such a condition will considerably influence the style of operation and limit capacity.

- Restrictions on the use of outside areas.

  Having a useable outside area, especially in the middle of a city, can boost sales enormously. They can also be a source of great concern to local residents who could disturbed by noise, especially later in the evening. Given this, it is commonplace to have a condition placed on a licence stating that it must close earlier than the premises as a whole. In extreme circumstances, gardens and terraces cannot be used at all for fear of disturbance. If the use of an outside area is important to a potential operator, they should have the ability to walk away if an overly restrictive condition is placed on a licence.

- A restriction on takeaways and/or off sales

  Takeaway delivery services have boomed in recent years. This has not necessarily been welcomed by people living close to restaurants which offer such a service. Mopeds can be noisy and having groups of delivery drivers outside a bedroom window talking and smoking can be intensely irritating. Hence, conditions restricted such activities are becoming more commonplace and, if essential to the business model, a prospective tenant might want the ability to look elsewhere if such conditions are imposed.

- Onerous capacity conditions.

  It is usually the case that a premises licence will not have a capacity condition as it is prescribed by the fire risk assessment unless necessary for safety reasons (i.e.

nightclub operations) or to prevent public nuisance. Certain council's, notably the City of Westminster, currently take a different view and may look to state capacities based on the number and location of fire escapes and the toilet provision. In respect of the latter this can often mean a much lower capacity is requested by Environmental Health than the number of covers that can reasonably be accommodated.

- An obligation to employ door supervisors (i.e. 'bouncers').

  Operators frequently employ door supervisors, not because a premises licence requires it, but because it is good practice. The role of the door supervisor has evolved from threatening 'hard man' to one which can direct queues, ensure that customers do not become overly noisy or wander into the wrong areas, control numbers and even brand ambassadors. Nevertheless, even if a premises employs door supervisors occasionally following a risk assessment they may not be happy with a condition that they have to be employed in certain numbers or at certain times. Not only can they be expensive to employ (door supervisors must be SIA registered) but they also give off a certain image. If an operator wants to open a quiet romantic restaurant, having a door supervisor employed gives the impression that it is lively bar.

- Having to use polycarbonate drinking vessels.

  If you are spending £75 on a bottle of champagne would you want to drink it from a plastic flute? The answer is probably 'no'. Hence any premises with such a condition cannot operate as an upmarket establishment.

- A condition imposing a requirement which cannot be complied with without the agreement of a third party.

  Again, another common onerous condition and, provided it is properly worded, usually a reasonable one. For example, having a condition which states that a premises can only open late on certain nights with the agreement of a local residents' group is fraught with danger. Having said that, imposed conditions which require agreement or input from a third-party public authority are common. CCTV might have to be installed as per the recommendations of the police, a sound limiter might have to set by environmental health etc.

- Any condition which, in the tenant's reasonable opinion, is onerous.

  It you are acting for a potential tenant, such a 'sweeper' provision is clearly desirable as it could relate to any number of conditions which could be deemed onerous but were not envisaged by the parties. Unsurprisingly, such an onerous condition should be resisted by a landlord. It is vague, too all encompassing and risks an Agreement for Lease becoming an Option Agreement.

Tenants will often seek to insert a general onerous condition such as, 'any condition which can impact upon the running of the business'. Such a condition should be resisted by landlords as this effectively transform the Agreement to Lease into an option.

- A prescribed timetable. To preserve momentum, the licensing provisions will normally have a prescribed timetable. This should be realistic. It can take a few weeks for accurate licensing plans to be drawn up. Not all licensing sub-committee hearings are convened within 20 working days of the last date for representations. A tenant cannot be certain that the grant of a premises licence will not be challenged until 21 days after the written decision notice has been received. If the Agreement for Lease allows or requires a tenant to appeal a refusal or grant of a premises licence with onerous condition, agreeing a longstop date is even more problematic. When any appeal can be heard depends on numerous factors: the complexity of the appeal, the number of witnesses, availability of experts, counsel, a judge and a court room. It is not unusual for appeals to take a year to be determined.

- Adequate supervision of the application process. Whilst a landlord will want any application to be made as expeditiously as possible, it will also be anxious to ensure that a sensible approach is being taken. Generally, the Agreement for Lease will provide that the landlord has to approve the premises licence application (such approval not be unrealistically withheld) and kept informed of any representations, hearing dates etc.

- A requirement that the landlord provides reasonable assistance. The licensing process should be a team effort. Landlords must accommodate the requirements of the application process including providing access in order that plans can be drawn up, the statutory authorities may visit and so the blue notice can be displayed.

- There should be a dispute resolution clause. Even with a detailed definition of what is, and is not, an onerous condition, disagreements do occur. Usually the dispute resolution clause refers disputes to a licensing barrister (or surveyor) of at least 10 years' experience.

What if I have no faith in the tenant's legal team to obtain a premises licence free of onerous conditions?

Whilst care must be taken to avoid a conflict of interest, the landlord can provide in the Agreement for Lease that it controls the application process to any degree desired. This could be anything from needing to approve the potential tenant's choice of licensing lawyer to applying for the premises licence on the tenant's behalf.

With a developer the approach is different. Can they risk years of construction and expense without the comfort of knowing that the local council would be prepared to grant a premises licence or licences? The Act provides for this – see paragraph 29. A developer can apply for a Provisional Statement which is essentially an outline premises licence. The application process mirrors that of an application for a new premises licence. The key difference is that a licensing plan is replaced by a schedule of work. If a provisional statement is granted, a subsequent application for a new premises licence is required. However, parties' abilities to make representations to the application for a new premises licence are limited provided that the application mirrors that of the provisional statement and the works described in the schedule of works accompanying the application have been satisfactorily completed. So far, so good.

Unfortunately, there are serious flaws with provisional statements. When applying for the subsequent premises licence, valid representations can still be made if:

- that person has a reasonable excuse as to why they did not object to the grant of a provisional statement; and
- there has been a material change in circumstances relating to the premises.

So, what does this mean? For example, it could be that an inner-city post-industrial site is being transformed over many years. Numerous provisional statements are granted early on with flats then being built and sold before the commercial units, including bars and restaurants are finally let. If those flats were bought and occupied after the provisional statements were granted but before premises licence applications were made those residents could raise representations. After all, when they bought their flats the surrounding area could have been very quiet only to become 'lively' once the first commercial units opened for business.

It is all very unsatisfactory. Whilst the provisional statement process is used, it does not provide as much comfort to developers as it should. There is an alternative. As explained in chapter 2, a broad range of businesses and entities can apply for a premises licence. A developer might be able to avoid having to apply for a provisional statement by applying for a premises licence instead. In such circumstances, a certain imagination is required. Plans will have to be drawn with the best 'guesstimate' as to how the final operation will look and, no doubt, the statutory authorities and other interested parties will want an idea as to the likely category of tenant. Even so, having a broadly suitable premises licence in place can avoid the requirement for an Agreement for Lease. Even if a subsequent application is required to vary the layout of the premises, in the main, these are not controversial.

How long in advance of opening can a premises licence be obtained?

There is no limit as to how long in advance of the proposed opening a premises licence can be granted. One of the authors had a premises licence granted for what was then a patch of sky. The existing building had yet to be knocked down following a compulsory purchase order and the new premises licence was only used five years later once the new development had been completed.

CHAPTER SIX
PRESERVATION OF AN ASSET

A unit with a premises licence can be a very valuable asset and hence worthy of careful preservation. As mentioned in previous chapters, premises licence can be fettered or lost either because of surrender, insolvency (as discussed in detail in chapter 4) or following a review application.

Premises licences can be surrendered by the licence holder if no longer required (for example if the premises is being demolished or changing its use). In such circumstances, anyone who is proposing to carry out licensable activities from those premises can reinstate the premises licence by way of a transfer application within 28 days. If this period has lapsed, a new premises licence must be applied for.

A responsible authority (usually the police, environmental health or the licensing authority itself) or any other person may apply to the local council to have a premises licence reviewed if they have concerns relating to the licensing objectives. This is a wide approach which could encompass anything from a serious stabbing in a nightclub to something as seemingly innocuous as early morning supplier deliveries. Provided that the application relates to one or more of the licensing objectives, review applications are only invalid if they are brought by someone other than a responsible authority (i.e. a local resident or neighbourhood group) and deemed to be 'frivolous', 'vexatious' or 'repetitious'. 'Repetitious' is deemed to be on the same ground more than once a year.

Are many review applications rejected for being frivolous or vexatious?

Not many are rejected by case officers who often prefer (understandably) for a licensing sub-committee to make such a decision. The difficulty is that an advocate cannot attend a review application licensing sub-committee hearing simply hoping that the application will be rejected on those grounds for fear that it will not and a substantive hearing immediately follows.

A review application can be very dangerous for a business. As with applications for new and variations to existing premises licences there is a 28-day consultation period during which other parties can have their say. A licensing sub-committee hearing is then convened within 20 working days. At that hearing, the very best an operator can hope for is that the sub-committee decides to take no action. In such circumstances *all* that has been lost is reputation, management time and money in the form of legal fees. The other options are far worse. The licensing sub-committee has the power to issue a formal warning, replace the designated premises supervisor, add conditions, cut hours, remove licensable activities, suspend the premises licence for up to 3 months or even revoke the licence altogether.

The more serious of these outcomes is not just a concern to the operator but also the landlord of the premises in question. Having a premises licence fettered or revoked could reduce the value of any reversion by hundreds of thousands of pounds. At review hearings, you often have the slightly bizarre situation whereby the landlord's advocate agrees with the reviewing party and argues for the strongest possible sanctions – even suspension – provided that the actual premises licence is not permanently compromised.

An even more serious summary review procedure was introduced in 2007 which allows the police to seek interim conditions, which could include closure within 48 hours of serious crime and disorder. In such circumstances, the first a landlord hears that there might be an issue is often when they read about it in the local press.

Can unfavourable review decisions be appealed?

They can and often are. Normal reviews are appealed not simply because the decision was unjust but because, if a decision is appealed, its effects are stayed until the appeal is heard. With a skilled legal team, availability (or lack therefore) of the parties involved and the pressure on court time it can takes months, if not over a year, before the appeal is heard. Also, the court will look at the operation of the premises at the time of the appeal, not original review. This gives operators time to rectify, where possible, any issues. The appeal process following an unfavourable summary review is complicated because, if the interim condition is that the premises should close, generally the premises will have to remain closed until the appeal is heard.

So how can a landlord ensure that its main asset is not compromised by a tenant surrendering the licence, causing it to lapse through death or insolvency or having it reviewed because it is failing to uphold the licensing objectives? There are several options:

Hold the premises licence itself

As explained in chapter 2, a landlord can hold a premises licence. Superficially this is an attractive option and one which was particularly favoured during years immediately following the introduction of the Act. The main advantage is that the premises licence will not lapse if the tenant dies or becomes insolvent and cannot be surrendered against the landlord's wishes. Also, whilst it will not prevent a review application being brought if the operator fails to uphold the licensing objectives, the landlord will at least be aware of the application and able to conduct the response if it considers that the operator and/or its legal team lack the requisite skill or interest.

The downsides, however, are significant. Unless the tenant is contractually bound to do so, the annual fee is payable by the landlord as the premises licence holder. Also, any applications pursuant to the Act (even TENs and Designated Premises Supervisor variations) will have to be made by the landlord. This results in increased administration and costs.

Apply for a 'shadow licence'

There is nothing in the Act which prevents multiple premises licences covering the same site. The intention of parliament was to permit different businesses or organisations to operate under the same roof. However, *Extreme Oyster Limited and Star Oyster Limited v Guildford Borough Council [2013] EWHC 2174 (Admin)* approved a more imaginative approach whereby a landlord can apply for second or 'shadow licence' on exactly the same terms as the principle licence which can be 'dusted down' if, for whatever reason, the principle licence ceases to be in force.

This approach has proved a godsend to many landlords of high-profile venues which have become insolvent. This is not only because a new tenant can operate immediately without having to wait the month, or two, for a new premises licence to be granted but also because there is no guarantee that a new premises licence would be granted on the same terms, if at all. Many late-night venues benefit from premises licence granted in more liberal times which, if applied for today, would be contrary to policy. Whilst some licensing policies look kindly on applications to reinstate lapsed licences, operations on the bring of financial ruin often 'push the boundaries' and incur the wrath of the police, environmental health and local residents alike. For a premises licence to have inadvertently lapsed for a troublesome nightclub is often seen as a blessing with attempts to reinstate it vigorously challenged.

The shadow licence approach is not necessarily quite as beneficial if the principle premises licence is reviewed. If the view is taken that the landlord should have supervised operations more proactively or that, no matter how well run the premises , the licensing objectives will suffer, then the aggrieved party might review both premises licences. Some sub-committees expect a landlord to take a very 'hands on' role to the running of their tenants' businesses and expect supervision to have been applied if the shadow licence is to escape the fate of the principle licence.

Furthermore, as is the case with holding the principle licence, having a shadow licence does require payment of an annual fee albeit this can be still be a very cost-effective way of protecting a very valuable asset.

Section 178 notification

The cost of applying for and maintaining a shadow licence can be inappropriate where the risk of the premises licence being lost is minimal or if it is easily replaceable. In such circumstances, a section 178 notification might be a sensible step. It gives the freeholder of a property a right, on request, to be informed of any application made in respect of the premises in question. This should provide 'early warning' of any application to surrender or review the premises licence in question. It is 'should' rather than 'will' because one is reliant on the council accurately recording and acting upon such notice. Also, any notice only has effect for 12 months, so notice applications must be repeated every year. Nevertheless, as the fee for each notification is only, at the time of writing, £21.00 it is a low-cost way of affording a landlord some element of protection.

Provisions in the lease

As an absolute minimum, there should be tenant's covenants in the lease which require it to inform the landlord if any complaints, review applications or prosecutions are brought. Whilst a practitioner could rightly be criticised for not incorporating such conditions, their effectiveness is questionable. In times of trouble it is rare for tenants to consult leases and, for obvious reasons, they might be wary of revealing the true extent of difficulties to the landlord.

CHAPTER SEVEN INTERACTION BETWEEN LICENSING AND PLANNING

There are many common misunderstandings when it comes to the relationship between licensing and planning.

Whilst planning is a separate regime and above and beyond the scope of this book the property practitioner needs to be aware of the basics of how the licensing and planning regimes interact.

Broadly speaking, an off-licence or shop should have an A1 use class, a restaurant A3, a bar or pub an A4, a takeaway A5 and a hotel C1. The correct use class for an operation is becoming ever more complicated and premises are used more imaginatively. For example, many wine shops have some covers for customers to drink inside and yet operate under A1, A3 restaurants have standalone bars which alone would be A4 and more primary cooking is done away from site to avoid the requirement to have A3 planning use. If there are doubts, advice should be sought from a specialist planning consultant. So, how does this affect licensing? Whilst they are separate regimes, many council licensing policies stipulate that the correct planning permission should be in place before a licensing application is made. If an application for a 'bar style' premises licence is made in respect of a premises which has an A1 use class this could draw the attention of the council's planning team and lead to enforcement action.

One regime does not 'trump' the other. Operators need to trade to whichever is the more restrictive. Premises licence and planning permissions do not necessarily mirror each other. However, whilst trading above and beyond that permitted by the premises licence is automatically a criminal offence, it is only a criminal offence to breach planning conditions if an enforcement notice is received and ignored.

Licensing and planning most commonly combine when looking at outside drinking.

Table and chairs licences

Table and chairs licences (also know as pavement or furniture licences) are required where an operator wishes to have furniture placed outside of the premises' curtilage, most commonly on the public pavement. The requirement for such permission is often overlooked but crucial given the direct and indirect revenue that having these additional covers provides.

The key legislation is the Highways Act 1980.This permits local councils to grant permission to place objects on the highway. The approach taken, and the fees charged, vary enormously between councils. There will be thousands of licensed premises throughout the county that have tables and chairs on the pavement without giving it any thought or paying the local council a penny. Other councils (especially ones in the large metropolitan areas have areas) inspect premises regularly and have detailed guidelines as to what is, and is not, permitted with hefty fees to boot. In some cases, planning permission is also required which might only be for a limited period.

If the outside area compromises the small square glass windows which illuminate a basement does this mean that it is within the demise of the building?

Not necessarily. Just because the basement protrudes under the outside pavement is does not mean the ground floor area above it also forms part of the demise.

CHAPTER EIGHT
OTHER CONSIDERATIONS

In addition to planning issues, there are other licences, laws and regulations which frequently go hand in hand with the matters governed by the Act. Here are some of them:

Registering as a Food Business

Every premises which carries out food operations, even if just on a mobile or temporary basis, must be registered as a food business at least 28 days before opening. It is a simple process conducted by the local authority in which the premises is located but one which is frequently overlooked. Failure to do so can lead to a fine and/or imprisonment.

Permission to play music

Separate to licensing requirements in the Act, most premises which play music will need to register with PPL and/or PRS and pay a licence fee.

Food safety

Food safety requirement is a vast and complex topic. Premises selling food will be inspected by the local authority after opening and awarded between zero and five stars with five stars being the highest standard.

Employment law

There are employment law issues which are unique to licensed venues in particular, the handling of tips, or TRONC as it is technically called. Clients should seek specialist advice if they are unsure of the rules. Operators also have a duty not to employ illegal immigrants. An operation which employs illegal immigrants can have its premises licence reviewed and revoked.

Smoking

Since 2007 smoking has been banned inside licensed premises. Smoking is only permitted under awnings or outside covered areas if 50% of the area remains open.

Sexual Entertainment Venues

In addition to requiring a premises licence, sexual entertainment venues also need a Sexual Establishment Licence. The approach to such venues varies from council to council. They do have the ability to limit the number in a locality and have wide powers to refuse the grant or annual renewal of such licences on grounds including the character of the locality and the layout, character and condition of the premises. Councils can come under significant pressure from residents and are heavily scrutinised to ensure that they do not breach conditions.

Noise Abatement

If noise is emanating from a licensed premises (for example, because of loud music, noisy plant or customers shouting in a beer garden) rather than, or addition to, seeking to review the premises licence, an Environmental Health Officer might serve a noise abatement notice. In such circumstances, the recipient of the notice can either comply with the notice or appeal. Failure to take either of these options could see a criminal prosecution being brought without further notice being given. There are a number of grounds on which noise abatement notices may be appealed, the most common being that service of the notice was not justified (i.e. there was no statutory nuisance) or that best practicable means were being used to prevent or counteract the effects of the nuisance. There is a 21 day period in which to appeal a noise abatement notice with no 'slip rule'.

Gambling

Governed by the Gambling Act 2005 ("2005 Act") all premises that offer gambling facilities (such as betting shops, bingo halls and arcades) require a 2005 Act premises licence as well as an Operating Licence granted by the UK Gambling Commission currently based in Birmingham.

In respect of 'bricks and mortar' gambling, the Act and 2005 Act share many similarities. The 2005 has its own licensing objectives and its premises licences can be varied, reviewed and transferred, hence the due diligence process when acquiring 2005 Act licensed premises will be familiar to anyone with knowledge of the Act. There are some important differences. For example, 2005 Act premises licences do not lapse following administration of the premises licence holder. Matters are complicated though by the requirement to have an Operating Licence. Operating Licences cannot be transferred and new applications are heavily scrutinised over many weeks, if not months, by the UK Gambling Commission.

Some premises will have both the Act and 2005 Act premises licences (such as bingo halls) whereas a pub with two or fewer gaming machines (i.e. 'fruit machines') are required to notify their local council whereas those with between two and four machines require a gaming machine permit which requires a formal application to be made to the local council.

Licensing in Scotland

The Licensing (Scotland) Act 2005 governs licensing in Scotland. It shares many similarities with the Act. However, two crucial differences are that every application is determined before a Licensing Board rather than being granted by way of delegated authority even if there are no objections and there is a fifth licensing objective: protecting and improving public health. It is fair to say that these differences and the general attitude to alcohol consumption in Scotland makes it more time consuming and difficult to get licences granted.

APPENDIX A
STANDARD PRE-CONTRACT ENQUIRES

Re: The Dog and Duck (the "Premises")

1. Please supply the following:

    1.1. Premises Licence;

    1.2. Any other Licences or consents relating or supplemental to the Premises Licence;

    1.3. Certificate confirming the safety of the electrical installations and emergency lighting and fire detection systems; and

    1.4. Any arrangements with the local authority in relation to the use of tables or seating on pavements outside the premises.

2. Please confirm that the Licence Holder and Designated Premises Supervisor are currently as quoted on the Licence and advise their present and future addresses for service of the Licensing Notices.

3. Please supply copy layout plans of the Premises which clearly define the Licensed areas.

4. Have all structural alterations made to the Premises received prior approval of the Licensing Authority and all

the relevant authorities including but not limited to the Fire Authority.

5. Has approval been given for any structural alterations, which have yet to be carried out? If so, then please supply full details together with copy plans.

6. Have any notices been received seeking review of the Premises Licence under the Licensing Act 2003 (and any subsequent legislation)?

7. Please confirm if any public or private entertainment is provided on the Premises and please specify the nature of that entertainment and both the days and the times at which it is provided.

8. Have the Licensees ever received warning from any party that proceedings may be taken to revoke the Licence or to prosecute any breach of its terms? If so, please supply copies.

9. Please confirm if any application for conversion of existing Licences for the premises was submitted during a transitional period and supply a copy of the application including the licences previously in force.

10. Since the Premises Licence was granted have there been any applications to vary the Licence? If so, please specify the outcome of any Applications made.

11. Please supply copies of all representations received as a result of any application to vary the Premises Licence.

12. As a result of any representations made, please confirm whether the Licensing Authority has held a hearing and, if so, confirm the outcome.

13. Please confirm that the Seller and all those persons working on the Premises have complied with the conditions as set out in the Licence.

14. Please confirm the full name and address of the Designated Premises Supervisor and confirm that he/she will remain as Designated Premises Supervisor until completion of this transaction.

15. Please confirm that the Designated Premises Supervisor will provide his/her consent to a variation of the Premises Licence to change the Designated Premises Supervisor.

16. 16 Please confirm that the Designated Premises Supervisor has not given notice to the Licensing Authority to be removed as the Designated Premises Supervisor for these Premises.

17. Has the Licence Holder received any correspondence or other intimation from responsible authorities or interested parties either threatening the possibility of an application for a review or serving as a warning that such action will be taken? If so, please supply details.

18. Please provide details of any convictions of either of the Licence Holder or any person working on the premises for any offences under the Licensing Act 2003 or Licensing Act 1964

19. Please confirm that no orders have been served for the closure of the licensed premises at any time. If such orders have been served, please supply copies.

20. Please confirm that the Holder of the Premises Licence and the Seller will consent to the transfer of the Premises Licence and that they will agree to the transfer having immediate effect from the date agreed for completion.

21. Where the premises are subject to a provisional statement, please supply a copy. Please also supply copies of any representations made by interested parties or responsible authorities at the time when the provisional statement was approved.

22. Please supply copies of all Temporary Event Notices submitted the premises user in the previous 12 months.

23. Please supply any Notices of Objection to Temporary Event Notices or any counter Notices from the Licensing Authority.

24. Please confirm that no Improvement Notices or Prohibition Notices have been served by the Local Authority under the Health & Safety Disability Discrimination Act, Building Regulations, Planning or other relevant legislation. If any such notices have been served then please supply copies.

25. Please confirm the hours during which hot food and hot drink is currently supplied to member of the public from the Premises.

26. Is there a Fire Certificate for the premises and, if so, please supply a copy. Further, please confirm that the conditions of the Fire Certificate have been complied with and that no alterations have been made to the Premises without the approval of the Fire Authority.

27. Has a permit been issued for the premises pursuant to Section 34 of the Gaming Act 1968? If so, please confirm the number of machines permitted and supply copies of the permits

28. If the gaming machines are the property of a third party, please supply detail of any hiring or other agreement and confirm that the Seller will use his best endeavours to ensure the transfer of the benefit of the agreement to the buyer if so requested.

29. Please confirm that there have never been any cases of food poisoning arising from food eaten or prepared at the premises. If there have been such cases, please supply details.

30. Please supply copies of any Notices served by Environmental Health Officers in connection with food safety or Statutory Notice.

31. Please provide details of any complaints from local residents or business regarding noise or any other issues arising from the conduct of the business.

32. Please supply details of any advanced bookings and confirm that any deposits will be transferred to the Buyer on completion.

33. Are all notices that are by law required to be displayed on the Premises currently displayed?

34. Please confirm there are no restrictive covenants or restrictions in any lease which restrict the sale of intoxicants or any other ancillary activity required for the use of the Premises.

35. Please confirm there is no application(s) pending for either transfer of the Premises Licence or to vary the Designated Premises Supervisor.

36. Please confirm that the Holder of the Premises Licence has not become bankrupt, insolvent or has or is about to enter into a form of administration or voluntary arrangement or has not or is about to be wound up.

37. Please confirm that all fees payable in respect of the Premises Licence have been paid and will continue to be made up to completion.

MORE BOOKS BY LAW BRIEF PUBLISHING

A selection of our other titles available now:-

'A Practical Guide to Vicarious Liability' by Mariel Irvine
'A Practical Guide to Claims Arising from Delays in Diagnosing Cancer' by Bella Webb
'A Practical Guide to Applications for Landlord's Consent and Variation of Leases' by Mark Shelton
'A Practical Guide to Relief from Sanctions Post-Mitchell and Denton' by Peter Causton
'Butler's Equine Tax Planning: 2nd Edition' by Julie Butler
'A Practical Guide to Equity Release for Advisors' by Paul Sams
'A Practical Guide to Immigration Law and Tier 1 Entrepreneur Applications' by Sarah Pinder
'A Practical Guide to Unlawful Eviction and Harassment' by Stephanie Lovegrove
'In My Backyard! A Practical Guide to Neighbourhood Plans' by Dr Sue Chadwick
'A Practical Guide to the Law Relating to Food' by Ian Thomas
'A Practical Guide to the Ending of Assured Shorthold Tenancies' by Elizabeth Dwomoh
'Commercial Mediation – A Practical Guide' by Nick Carr
'A Practical Guide to Financial Services Claims' by Chris Hegarty
'The Law of Houses in Multiple Occupation: A Practical Guide to HMO Proceedings' by Julian Hunt
'A Practical Guide to Unlawful Eviction and Harassment' by Stephanie Lovegrove
'A Practical Guide to Solicitor and Client Costs' by Robin Dunne
'Artificial Intelligence – The Practical Legal Issues' by John Buyers
'A Practical Guide to Wrongful Conception, Wrongful Birth and Wrongful Life Claims' by Rebecca Greenstreet

'Occupiers, Highways and Defective Premises Claims: A Practical Guide Post-Jackson – 2nd Edition' by Andrew Mckie
'A Practical Guide to Financial Ombudsman Service Claims' by Adam Temple & Robert Scrivenor
'A Practical Guide to the Law of Enfranchisement and Lease Extension' by Paul Sams
'A Practical Guide to Marketing for Lawyers – 2nd Edition' by Catherine Bailey & Jennet Ingram
'A Practical Guide to Advising Schools on Employment Law' by Jonathan Holden
'Certificates of Lawful Use and Development: A Guide to Making and Determining Applications' by Bob Mc Geady & Meyric Lewis
'A Practical Guide to the Law of Dilapidations' by Mark Shelton
'A Practical Guide to the 2018 Jackson Personal Injury and Costs Reforms' by Andrew Mckie
'A Guide to Consent in Clinical Negligence Post-Montgomery' by Lauren Sutherland QC
'A Practical Guide to Running Housing Disrepair and Cavity Wall Claims: 2nd Edition' by Andrew Mckie & Ian Skeate
'A Practical Guide to the General Data Protection Regulation (GDPR)' by Keith Markham
'A Practical Guide to Digital and Social Media Law for Lawyers' by Sherree Westell
'A Practical Guide to Holiday Sickness Claims – 2nd Edition' by Andrew Mckie & Ian Skeate
'A Practical Guide to Inheritance Act Claims by Adult Children Post-Ilott v Blue Cross' by Sheila Hamilton Macdonald
'A Practical Guide to Elderly Law' by Justin Patten
'Arguments and Tactics for Personal Injury and Clinical Negligence Claims' by Dorian Williams
'A Practical Guide to QOCS and Fundamental Dishonesty' by James Bentley
'A Practical Guide to Drone Law' by Rufus Ballaster, Andrew Firman, Eleanor Clot
'Practical Mediation: A Guide for Mediators, Advocates, Advisers, Lawyers, and Students in Civil, Commercial, Business, Property, Workplace, and Employment Cases' by Jonathan Dingle with John Sephton

'Practical Horse Law: A Guide for Owners and Riders' by Brenda Gilligan
'A Comparative Guide to Standard Form Construction and Engineering Contracts' by Jon Close
'A Practical Guide to Compliance for Personal Injury Firms Working With Claims Management Companies' by Paul Bennett
'A Practical Guide to the Landlord and Tenant Act 1954: Commercial Tenancies' by Richard Hayes & David Sawtell
'A Practical Guide to Personal Injury Claims Involving Animals' by Jonathan Hand
'A Practical Guide to Psychiatric Claims in Personal Injury' by Liam Ryan
'Introduction to the Law of Community Care in England and Wales' by Alan Robinson
'A Practical Guide to Dog Law for Owners and Others' by Andrea Pitt
'Ellis and Kevan on Credit Hire – 5th Edition' by Aidan Ellis & Tim Kevan
'RTA Allegations of Fraud in a Post-Jackson Era: The Handbook – 2nd Edition' by Andrew Mckie
'RTA Personal Injury Claims: A Practical Guide Post-Jackson' by Andrew Mckie
'On Experts: CPR35 for Lawyers and Experts' by David Boyle
'An Introduction to Personal Injury Law' by David Boyle
'A Practical Guide to Claims Arising From Accidents Abroad and Travel Claims' by Andrew Mckie & Ian Skeate
'A Practical Guide to Cosmetic Surgery Claims' by Dr Victoria Handley
'A Practical Guide to Chronic Pain Claims' by Pankaj Madan
'A Practical Guide to Claims Arising from Fatal Accidents' by James Patience
'A Practical Approach to Clinical Negligence Post-Jackson' by Geoffrey Simpson-Scott
'A Practical Guide to Personal Injury Trusts' by Alan Robinson
'Employers' Liability Claims: A Practical Guide Post-Jackson' by Andrew Mckie
'A Practical Guide to Subtle Brain Injury Claims' by Pankaj Madan
'The Law of Driverless Cars: An Introduction' by Alex Glassbrook
'A Practical Guide to Costs in Personal Injury Cases' by Matthew Hoe